DBC Creative Consulting
www.dbccreativeconsulting.ca
Ontario, Canada

Copyright © Mind Your Divorce: Empowering Women Through Separation & Divorce, 2022

All Rights Reserved. Without limiting the rights under copyright reserved above, no part of this publication may be reproduced, stored in, or introduced into a retrieval system, or transmitted in any form or by any means (electronic, mechanical, including photocopying, recording or otherwise), without the prior written permission of both the copyright owner and the above publisher of this book.

This publication contains the opinions and ideas of its author and is designed to provide useful information in regard to the subject matter covered. The author and publisher are not engaged in health or other professional services in this publication. This publication is not intended to provide a basis for action in particular circumstances without consideration by a competent professional. The author and publisher expressly disclaim any responsibility for any liability, loss, or risk, personal or otherwise, which is incurred as a consequence, directly or indirectly, of the use and application of any of the contents of this book. While the author has made every effort to provide accurate information at publication time, the publisher and the author assume no responsibility for author or third-party websites or their content.

Cornibert, Donna
Mind Your Divorce: Empowering Women Through Separation & Divorce

Paperback ISBN 978-1-7779738-0-3

Nonfiction | Body, Mind & Spirit | Mindfulness & Meditation
Nonfiction | Self-Help | Personal Growth | Success
Nonfiction | Self-Help | Motivational & Inspirational

This book is sold subject to the condition that it shall not, by way of trade or otherwise, be lent, re-sold, hired out, or otherwise circulated without the publisher's prior consent in any form of binding or cover other than that in which it is published and without a similar condition including this condition being imposed on the subsequent purchase.

Dedication

To my five children: Cameron, Tate, Zachary, Summer, and Olivia. You have been a constant blessing in my life.

To my best friend, my Mum, who showed me how to be a strong woman, and my Dad (who sadly passed away before I had a chance to realize this book), who were always there for me during my divorce.

And for all those women out there who are about to embark on the next chapter of their lives.

Donna

Donation

From every book sold, I will be donating 10% to a women's shelter in Canada. I was fortunate enough to have been able to keep a roof over my, and my children's, head during my divorce and I am so grateful for that, but I realized firsthand while going through this process how difficult it can be for some women to gain access to money if their finances are being controlled by their partner. The legal system doesn't account for this, which was shocking to me. This means so many women end up having to stay in abusive situations until they can find the means to get out or get a place in a women's shelter. It shouldn't be this way.

Introduction

It took four long years to finally get through my Separation and Divorce. Who'd have thought it would take so long, but it did. And to say that I am actually very grateful for all the lessons I learned during this period may seem a little warped...but I am. I have grown and developed so much as a person, and I wouldn't be as happy as I am or in the amazing place that I am today if I didn't go through this and learn these lessons. Now, you may be wondering what lessons are worth going through all this stress, anxiety, and pain for? Well, first and foremost, learning to accept responsibility for the part that I played in the end of my marriage. It's a bitter pill to swallow, but the fact is, it takes two to tango. I am not saying that if you are being abused that you asked to be (whether emotionally, physically, mentally, or financially) because obviously any form of abuse is unacceptable, and the abuser has definite issues that need to be dealt with. What we have to look at is why we end up with these types of partners, why we allow ourselves to be treated in certain ways, and where our sense of worth, or worthlessness, comes from because we make the conscious decision to be with them. It is our choice and life will keep sending us lessons until we actually learn from them.

I often think about my childhood, and how it played a role in my marriage. I grew up in London, England, of mixed parentage...a white mum and a black dad, during a time when mixed relationships were not accepted and completely frowned upon. Even though I grew up in Nottinghill Gate, a melting pot of cultures, I always felt that I came from something that was forbidden. It was normal to be referred to as 'half caste' (basically half of a person), coloured, or told that my dad was a 'coon'. Being so light-skinned and green-eyed, no one ever realized that I was mixed race. This meant that quite often I would end up in situations that were really uncomfortable, with people make derogatory comments about black people, not realizing that I was actually half black. I would just sit quietly and not say a word; I was too scared. I felt as though I was in a world where on the surface it looked as though I belonged, but underneath I didn't. As a teenager, my mum would tell me that if I dated any white boys to make sure that they knew I had a black dad to save on any heartache down the line, in case they decided they didn't want to be with me as a result. I know my mum loved me so much and was only trying to protect me by saying this, but this made me feel as though there was something wrong with me and that I was a creation of something that wasn't acceptable. I would ask boys if they minded that I was half black. Thinking back to this now, all I can say is...wow! This is exactly where my feelings of worthlessness came from. These feelings of not being enough eventually filtered into my future relationships and finally my marriage, which sadly ended in a long, drawn-out divorce.

Through this whole process I learned to let go of the pain that I was holding onto and found ways to cope with the stress and anxiety. With a newfound freedom, I was able to get back to being me and doing things that I used to love...like being creative without being told I was wasting my time. There were evenings when my youngest daughter would ask me to sit down and colour with her. This helped me take my mind off the day and de-stress. I started to notice how calming it was. I studied Art and Design at Chelsea College of Art and Textile Design at Central St Martins as well as completing a BSc in Psychology at Bath University. I was actually contemplating pursuing a career in Art Therapy by merging the two disciplines. It's funny how life leads you back to the path you were meant to be on!

This made me think about how amazing it would be to create something to help other women going through the same thing I did. When you colour, you go over and over the same spot quite a few times, so I thought that creating affirmations within a piece of art would reinforce the message as it was coloured. Sometimes we have to tell ourselves things over and over again before we believe them. Hence, my purpose for creating this colouring book...to help you mindfully get through your divorce and reinforce how amazingly strong, beautiful, and worthy YOU ARE...yes, YOU! Divorce doesn't have to be negative, it's actually a beautiful time for transformation. You now have an opportunity to realize your strengths, be who you were meant to be, and, in turn, find your purpose. Take time out of each day to use this book and the affirmations will be reinforced as you colour every page. Inspirational quotes will help you realize that you have the strength and courage to get through each and every day. Then, write a note to yourself on the journal page to relate each quote to your own life. You have so got this!

We shouldn't worry first about whether someone will love us for who we are; we have to start with learning to love ourselves first rather than conceding for anything less than we deserve. This has been a huge life lesson for me, and I want to share this journey with you through this book. I have learned to let go of other people's ideas of who I was or should be. I no longer feel stuck and can finally be ME! Learning to love yourself wholly and unconditionally will bring someone to you who will in turn love you for being your AUTHENTIC SELF, not who they want you to be. And just in case at any time you start to doubt yourself, you should know that...

You are STRONG,
You are WORTHY,
You are BEAUTIFUL,
You are BRAVE,
You are LOVED,
You are YOU, and that is far more than ENOUGH.

Today, is the start of a new chapter. Are you ready? Let's go!

About the Author

Donna Cornibert grew up in Notting Hill Gate, in the cultural melting pot that is London, UK. Of mixed white and black parentage, her fondest memories are of going shopping on a Saturday morning along Portobello Road with her mum, buying their groceries from the fruit and vegetable market stalls. The sights, sounds and smells of all the different cultures from her childhood are what has inspired her unconventionalism, love of everything different and not wanting to follow the 'norm'. Donna holds a BTEC National Diploma in Art & Design from Chelsea College of Art, a BSc Honors Degree in Psychology from Bath University and a PGDip/MA in Textile Design from Central Saint Martins College of Art & Design. She has been a floor manager and producer for television, press officer, assistant editor, photographer and stylist, entrepreneur, personal trainer, Pilates instructor and mother.

Donna has built up her photography business in the last two years shooting over 50 'Doorstep Dancers' and family shoots for charity in collaboration with the REACH Foundation and the Oakville Community Foundation. She is now the CEO of her own creative consulting company. Having five children and using photography to capture all their beautiful life moments, Donna realized that this was her true joy. She lives by the mantra, "Do what you love, follow your joy, serve others and you will find happiness and success!"

Be proud of yourself for how far you have come.

<u>Note to Self:</u>
I am proud of myself because...

"You are enough. You are so enough. It is unbelievable how enough you are." Sierra Boggess

<u>Note to Self:</u>
I am enough...

"Everything is hard before it is easy."
Johann Wolfgang von Goethe

Note to Self:
It will get easier when...

"Everything is hard before it is easy."

Flowers need time to bloom, so do you.

<u>Note to Self:</u>

If I were a flower, I would be a...

Flowers need time to bloom, so do you.

Remember, some things have to end for better things to begin.

Note to Self:
What things are ending? How do they make way for better?

Do what's best for you and do it at your own pace.

<u>Note to Self:</u>
what is best for me?

Prioritize your peace.

<u>Note to Self:</u>
I prioritize my peace by...

You are complete on your own.

<u>Note to Self:</u>
These are the things that complete me...

Change is uncomfortable but necessary.

<u>Note to Self:</u>
I am changing by...

Change is uncomfortable but necessary.

"I didn't come this far to only come this far."
Tom Brady

<u>Note to Self:</u>
I have accomplished...

"I didn't come this far to only come this far."
Tom Brady

Stop waiting for everything to be perfect to be happy.

<u>Note to Self:</u>
What things make me happy Right Now?

You are not responsible for things you can't control.

<u>Note to Self:</u>
These are the things I can control...

You are not responsible for things you can't control.

"Life isn't about finding yourself. It's about creating yourself." George Bernard Shaw

<u>Note to Self:</u>
I create myself every day by...

"Life isn't about finding yourself. It's about creating yourself." George Bernard Shaw

Be proud of yourself. You've been through so much and, despite it all, you're still pushing forward.

<u>Note to Self:</u>
I am still pushing forward by...

There's a future version of me who's proud I was strong enough.

<u>Note to Self:</u>

I am strong enough to handle...

Be yourself. Accept yourself. Love yourself. Empower yourself.

<u>Note to Self:</u>
I love and accept myself for...

Don't force yourself to want what
doesn't want you back.

<u>Note to Self:</u>

I will not force myself to...

Don't force yourself to want what
doesn't want you back.

"Your opinion is not my reality." Steve Maraboli

<u>Note to Self:</u>
My reality includes...

"Your opinion is not my reality." Steve Maraboli

You are allowed to outgrow people.

<u>Note to Self:</u>
The people in my life that bring positivity and growth are...

You are allowed to outgrow people.

Keep doing your best. You are trying and that is ENOUGH.

<u>Note to Self:</u>

I am doing my best every day to...

Never confuse what you are offered with what you are worth.

<u>Note to Self:</u>

I deserve...

Never confuse what you are offered with what you are worth.

Stand in your truth even if it means standing alone.

Note to Self:
My truth is...

Stand in your truth even if it means standing alone.

Your future needs you. Your past doesn't.

> Note to Self:
> My future will look like...

Your future needs you. Your past doesn't.

Some stuff just isn't worth your energy. Learn to pick and choose your battles.

<u>Note to Self:</u>

I choose positive energy by...

Putting yourself first isn't selfish, it's responsible.

Note to Self:
I put myself first when...

Putting yourself first isn't selfish, it's responsible.

I can and I will. watch me.

Note to Self:
I will accomplish...

I can and I will. watch me.

Remind yourself: people leave, life goes on, it is what it is, everything is temporary, don't over think, and let it go!

<u>Note to Self:</u>
I will let go of anything that holds me back...

Respect yourself enough to say, "I deserve better."

Note to Self:
I deserve...

Respect yourself enough to say, "I deserve better."

Whatever didn't work out wasn't meant for you.
Trust the process.

<u>Note to Self:</u>

I will trust the process by...

Whatever didn't work out wasn't meant for you.

Don't shrink yourself for other people's comfort.

> Note to Self:
> I will stop shrinking myself when...

Don't shrink yourself for other people's comfort.

Focus on things you can control.

Note to Self:
I can control...

Focus on things you can control.

You can never lose anything that isn't meant for you.

<u>Note to Self:</u>
These things were not meant for me...

You can never lose anything that isn't meant for you.

"Breathe, darling. This is just a chapter. It's not your whole story." S.C. Lourie

<u>Note to Self:</u>
I will practice breathing when...

"Breathe, darling. This is just a chapter. It's not your whole story." S.C. Lourie

Remember: Difficult does not mean impossible.

Note to Self:
These things are difficult but not impossible...

It's time for you to choose yourself.

Note to Self:
I choose myself by...

It's time for you to choose yourself.

Try to find the positive when surrounded by negativity.

<u>Note to Self:</u>
I focus on positivity by...

There is happiness in letting go.

Note to Self:
I am happy...

There is happiness in letting go.

Don't abandon yourself. Protect yourself.
Take care of yourself.

Note to Self:
I practice self care by...

Don't abandon yourself. Protect yourself. Take care of yourself.

If protecting yourself is selfish, then so be it.

<u>Note to Self:</u>
I protect myself when...

Try to appreciate where you are now.

Note to Self:

I appreciate the now...

Try to appreciate where you are now.

Embrace change. Trust your journey. Enjoy the view.

<u>Note to Self:</u>

I embrace change...

Embrace change. Trust your journey. Enjoy the view.

"It doesn't take a lot of strength to hang on. It takes a lot of strength to let go." J.C. Watts Jr.

<u>Note to Self:</u>
I believe I am strong...

"She believed she could, so she did." R.S. Grey

<u>Note to Self:</u>
I believe I can...

Because this will wreck you, it will actually make you stronger.

<u>Note to Self:</u>
I won't let it wreck me...

Because this will wreck you, it will actually make you stronger.

She chooses herself because you refuse to.

<u>Note to Self:</u>
I choose myself...

She chooses herself because you refuse to.

"The comeback is always stronger than the setback."
Dr. Jill Murray

<u>Note to Self:</u>
My comebacks include...

You're a diamond, dear. They can't break you.

<u>Note to Self:</u>

I am a diamond because...

You're a diamond, dear. They can't break you.

She promised herself better and never looked back.

<u>Note to Self:</u>
I will no longer look back at...

She promised herself better and never looked back.

Learn to be done. Not mad, not bothered, just done.

<u>Note to Self:</u>
I'm so done with...

Learn to be done. Not mad, not bothered, just done.

Don't let the concept of change scare you as much as the concept of staying unhappy.

<u>Note to Self:</u>

I will no longer be scared of...

How your life feels is more important than how it looks.

<u>Note to Self:</u>

I feel my life...

How your life feels is more important than how it looks.

"She remembered who she was and the game changed."
Lalah Delia

Note to Self:
I am a game changer...

"She remembered who she was and the game changed."

Girl, YOU already have what it takes.

Note to Self:
I have what it takes to...

Girl, YOU already have what it takes.

I deserve LOVE, I deserve SELF CARE, I deserve RESPECT, I deserve HONESTY, I deserve THE BEST, I deserve TO BE NOTICED, I deserve TO GET BETTER.

<u>Note to Self:</u>
My inner voice is telling me...

You are strong enough to face it all, even if it doesn't feel like it right now.

Note to Self:
I can face it all...

You are strong enough to face it all, even if it doesn't feel like it right now.

We FALL. We BREAK. We FAIL. But then...We RISE. We HEAL. We OVERCOME.

Note to Self:

I am overcoming...

We FALL. We BREAK. We FAIL. But then...We RISE. We HEAL. We OVERCOME.

I trust the next chapter, because I know the author.

<u>Note to Self:</u>
I am the author of my life...

I trust the next chapter, because I know the author.

"Evolving involves eliminating." Erykah Badu

<u>Note to Self:</u>
I am always evolving...

"Evolving involves eliminating." Erykah Badu

No one is YOU and that is YOUR SUPERPOWER.

Note to Self:
My superpowers are...

I'm doing this for ME.

Note to Self:
This is my time to...

I'm doing this for ME.

Keep taking time for yourself until you are YOU again.

<u>Note to Self:</u>

I take time for myself...

Just because a decision hurts, doesn't mean it's the wrong decision.

<u>Note to Self:</u>
All decisions move me forward...

Never forget that you deserve to be loved and respected.

Note to Self:
I respect myself...

Babe, learn to be okay with people not knowing your side of the story. You have nothing to prove to anyone.

<u>Note to Self:</u>
I have nothing to prove...

The more you love your decisions, the less you need others to love them.

> Note to Self:
> I love my decisions...

Remember, when you forgive, you heal.

<u>Note to Self:</u>
I forgive to heal...

When you let go, you grow.

<u>Note to Self:</u>

I am growing everyday...

"If you are still looking for that one person who will change your life, take a look in the mirror." Roman Price

<u>Note to Self:</u>
Only I can change my life...

You are not in control of which lessons others are here to learn.

> Note to Self:
> I am here to learn...

You are not in control of which lessons others are here to learn.

REPEAT AFTER ME: I'm allowed to do what's best for me, even if it upsets people.

Note to Self:
I do what's best for me by...

You have no idea how good life is going to get for you.

> **Note to Self:**
> Life is only going to get better...

You have no idea how good life is going to get for you.

Make yourself your priority. At the end of the day, you're your longest commitment.

<u>Note to Self:</u>

I am committed to me...

You become extremely powerful once you learn to control how you react.

<u>Note to Self:</u>

I am powerful...

It's time to forgive yourself. You're not that person anymore.

<u>Note to Self:</u>
I forgive myself for...

It's time to forgive yourself. You're not that person anymore.

And she continued... a SUCCESSFUL WOMAN.

Note to Self:
I am successful...

And she continued... a SUCCESSFUL WOMAN.

The best advice I was given: Move on if you're tired of waiting, and they can catch up to you if they miss you.

<u>Note to Self:</u>

I am moving on...

"The vibration of being who you are and doing what you love is magnetic." Maryam Hasnaa

<u>Note to Self:</u>

I am doing me...

"You will align everything you need in your life with [your] energy." Maryam Hasnaa

<u>Note to Self:</u>
I am aligned with my perfect life...

A beautiful day begins with a beautiful mindset.

Note to Self:
Life is beautiful...

A beautiful day begins with a beautiful mindset.

www.ingramcontent.com/pod-product-compliance
Lightning Source LLC
Chambersburg PA
CBHW081709100526
44590CB00022B/3710